MATERIALS THAT MATTER

GLASS

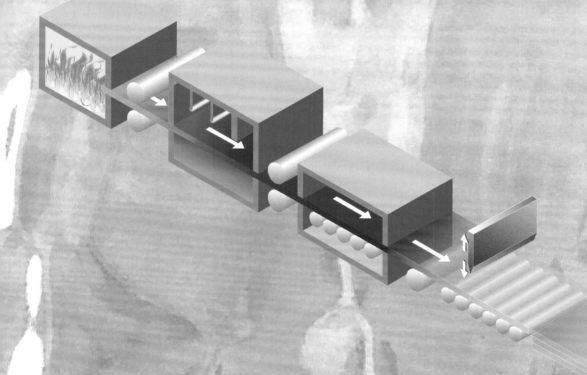

Neil Morris

W
FRANKLIN WATTS
LONDON•SYDNEY

An Appleseed Editions book

First published in 2010 by Franklin Watts
338 Euston Road, London NW1 3BH

Franklin Watts Australia
Hachette Children's Books
Level 17/207 Kent St, Sydney, NSW 2000

© 2010 Appleseed Editions

Created by Appleseed Editions Ltd,
Well House, Friars Hill, Guestling,
East Sussex TN35 4ET

Designed by Helen James
Edited by Mary-Jane Wilkins
Artwork by Graham Rosewarne
Picture research by Su Alexander

ISBN 978 1 4451 0020 3

Dewey Classification: 620.1'44

A CIP catalogue for this book is available from the British Library.

Photograph acknowledgements
page 4 D.Hurst/Alamy; 5 Croftsphoto/Alamy; 6 LeighSmithImages/Alamy;
7 Werner Forman/Corbis; 8 Imagestate Media Partners Ltd-Impact Photos/
Alamy; 9 JTB Photo Communications, Inc/Alamy; 10 Wallace Weeks/Alamy;
12 ImageState/Alamy; 13 Neil Morris; 14 Catherine Benson/Reuters/Corbis;
15 Pat Behnke/Alamy; 16 Cephas Picture Library/Alamy; 17 Massimo Listri/
Corbis; 18 Piotr Powietrzynski/Alamy; 19 Jack Sullivan/Alamy; 20 Alain
Nogues/Corbis Sygma; 21 Suzanne Long/Alamy; 22 Pablo Paul/Alamy;
24 Ashley Cooper/Alamy; 25 Mark Sykes/Alamy; 26 Bubbles Photolibrary/
Alamy; 27 Philip Scalia/Alamy; 28 Kirsty McLaren/Alamy; 29 Timelinks.org
Front cover Mark Zylber/Alamy

Printed in China

Franklin Watts is a division of Hachette Children's Books,
an Hachette UK company.
www.hachette.co.uk

Contents

What is glass?

Everyone knows what glass looks like, although it can be hard to see. That's because most glass is transparent, or see-through. Glass is usually brittle, which means that it's hard but breaks easily. If you knock a drinking glass to the floor, it might smash into little pieces. But there are many different types of glass, including toughened kinds that hardly break at all.

Glass can be moulded into all sorts of shapes. It is also practical. This glassware can easily be seen by shoppers through the glass window.

Main ingredients

You can find natural glass rocks, such as **obsidian**, which is a dark shiny rock made from lava (see page 6). These rocks are sometimes called volcanic glass. But the everyday glass we know is made by mixing various ingredients together. The main one is silica sand. The scientific name for it is **silicon dioxide**, because it contains the elements silicon and oxygen. The other ingredients are **soda ash** (sodium carbonate) and **limestone** (calcium carbonate). These help the mixture to melt more easily when it is heated, and they make glass harder when it cools. Most of the world's manufactured glass is soda-lime glass.

Heating and shaping

To make soda-lime glass, the mixture of minerals is heated in a **furnace** to a very high temperature. The mixture melts at about 1500°C (15 times hotter than the boiling

USE IT AGAIN AND AGAIN

Many types of glass can be used again and again (see pages 26-27). It is impossible to tell whether a glass bottle is newly made or recycled. Every time bottles and jars are recycled, the environment benefits. For every tonne of glass recycled rather than made from new ingredients:

• 345 kWh less energy is used;
• 315 kg less CO_2 (**carbon dioxide**) is given off;
• 1.2 tonnes less raw materials are used;
• 1 tonne less glass goes to a landfill rubbish dump.

SPECIAL SOLID

Glass is a solid material. It keeps its shape and doesn't flow like a liquid, which is runny. We make glass by cooling molten – or very hot liquid – substances quickly. Because of this, glass is similar to a liquid in some ways.

point of water). The molten glass is shaped into sheets or containers. Craftsmen do this using their hands and mouths (see page 10) but in factories the glass is prepared and shaped by machines (see page 12).

A huge pile of silica sand sits outside a glass factory. Sand is dug from quarries and transported to the factory by rail or road.

The first glass

Volcanic glass called obsidian forms when red-hot lava from an erupting volcano cools very quickly. The glassy rock is not transparent but black, or sometimes a reddish colour. In prehistoric times people chipped off pieces of obsidian and used them as cutting and piercing tools. Flakes of volcanic glass made very sharp knives and spearheads.

Then people started using obsidian for decoration. At least 7000 years ago it was used in Mesopotamia (present-day Iraq) to make jewellery and drinking **vessels**. Later, the ancient Greeks used it to make mirrors.

Legendary beginnings

There are several stories about how the first glass was made. They are all based on a chance discovery, but we do not know whether they are true stories or legends. A Roman scholar called Pliny the Elder (AD 23-79) wrote about a group of Phoenician sailors who moored their boat on a sandy beach and cooked a meal nearby. They put their cooking pots on blocks of **saltpetre** from their cargo and made a fire underneath with wood. After their meal, when the fire died down, the sailors were amazed to discover that the sand

This piece of obsidian was shaped into a spearhead in ancient times.

These glass perfume flasks were made in ancient Egypt more than 3000 years ago.

underneath the fire had turned into a shiny material – glass.

A medieval Saxon scientist called Georg Agricola (1494-1555) wrote a similar story in a famous book on metals and other materials.

Pots and beads

About 5000 years ago, craftsmen used glass to add a shiny finish – called a glaze – to pottery. **Archaeologists** have found glass beads which may be even older than the glazed pottery. Around 1600 BC, craftsmen in Mesopotamia and ancient Egypt made glass vessels. They shaped their vessels by moulding a core of mud into the shape they wanted the inside of the vessel to be. They dipped this in glass they had melted

in a furnace, and allowed it to cool before scraping out the mud core. Archaeologists have found several glass-working sites in Egypt, including one in the famous city of El-Amarna.

RECYCLE RECYCLE RECYCLE RECYCLE

Venice and Murano

The ancient Egyptians probably made the first glass. The blowpipe was invented later, during the first century BC, along the eastern Mediterranean coast, where the country of Syria is today. It is still used today. A craftsman gathered molten glass on the end of a hollow pipe. Then he blew through the pipe to form a glass bubble that could be shaped into a vessel.

Growing in importance

Syria fell to the Romans in 64 BC, and glass-making quickly spread through the Roman Empire. By AD 1224 there was a **guild** (or trade association) of glass makers in Venice. Before the end of the thirteenth century, all the glass makers moved to the Venetian island of Murano. This reduced the risk of the glass furnaces setting fire to Venice's wooden buildings. The industry was so important that glass makers became honoured Venetian citizens. They were not allowed to leave in case they gave away the secrets of Murano glass making.

Master craftsmen

By 1600, almost half the 7000 people who lived on Murano were involved in glass making. Master craftsmen developed new techniques, which made Murano glass famous. They started making many different kinds of glass, including:

- clear and sparkling **crystalline glass**;
- enamelled glass, using coloured glass powder;
- multicoloured glass, called in Italian *millefiori* (meaning a thousand flowers);
- **opaque** white glass called *latticinio* (meaning milk food);
- fine glass beads used as imitation **gemstones** in jewellery.

A Murano glass maker rolls and shapes a lump of molten glass using traditional methods that have lasted for centuries.

Murano today

Today tourists visit the Museum of Glass in the Giustinian Palace on the island. There are also demonstrations of glass-blowing and many shops sell Murano glass objects. Visitors can buy drinking glasses, ornaments, **figurines**, beads, **chandeliers** and mirrors.

Stained glass

Stained-glass windows became an important part of the design of medieval cathedrals and churches. Craft workers made sheets of coloured glass by adding **oxides** to the mixture. The oxides came from metal ores: cobalt oxide was added to make blue glass, copper for red, manganese for purple and iron oxide for yellow.

The glass makers cut the coloured sheets into small pieces, which were fitted together inside lead strips to make up a picture.

This stained-glass window in Chartres Cathedral, France, was made about 1180. It shows the Virgin Mary seated on a throne with Jesus on her lap surrounded by angels.

They used black glassy enamel to add details, and an iron window frame held the strips together. Light shining through the stained glass made the images glow.

RESTORING HISTORY

RESTORE RESTORE RESTORE RESTORE

Experts can restore old stained-glass windows, even when pieces of the glass are damaged or in poor condition. Victorian houses often had stained glass in or above their front doors. This can be reused elsewhere when new doors are fitted.

Modern glass-making

Today there are many ways of making glassware. Some is made traditionally; handmade glasses are made in the same way as they were centuries ago. Some modern materials are purer, the glass clearer, and modern furnaces more efficient. Newer techniques for making sheets of glass have been developed in recent times.

Gathering and blowing

To blow glass, a glass-blower first gathers molten glass on the end of a long metal pipe. He rolls the glass on a metal plate, then raises the pipe and blows through it to make an air-filled bubble of glass. Great skill and years of experience are needed to blow and twist the glass, stretching and squeezing it into shape. This can be done very quickly, and sometimes the glass-blower may reheat the glass to keep it soft. He may also use a hollow **mould** to form the basic shape. Then he might pull out a knob of glass to make a stem, or add a **gob** of glass for a handle. The work has to be done while the glass is still soft and sticky.

This craftsman is blowing through the pipe to shape the runny glass.

Flattening glass

Early flat sheets of glass were made by moulding the glass into discs or cylinders and then flattening it. Later, pools of molten glass and rollers were used to make thin sheet glass, which was then ground and polished. During the 1950s a British industrialist named Alastair Pilkington (1920-95) invented a new technique. This was called the float-glass method, and it is

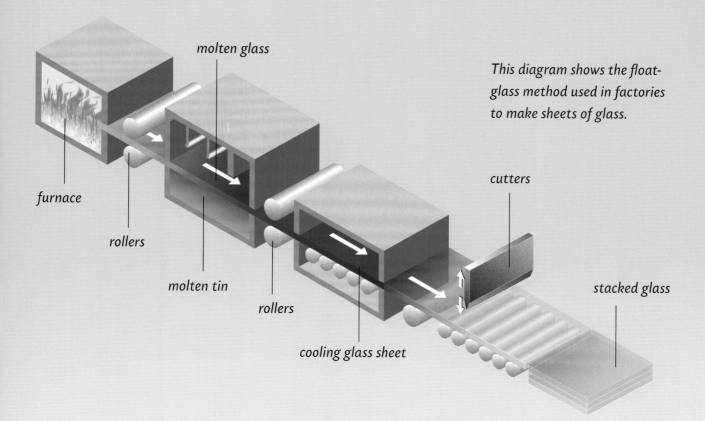

molten glass

furnace

rollers

molten tin

rollers

cooling glass sheet

cutters

stacked glass

This diagram shows the float-glass method used in factories to make sheets of glass.

used everywhere today. In Pilkington's float-glass method, molten glass is poured over a smooth surface of molten tin, where the glass spreads and hardens into a continuous ribbon, or strip. The ribbon of glass is usually about seven millimetres thick, but it can be compressed to make thicker plate glass or stretched to make thinner sheets. Once it has cooled, the ribbon of glass is cut into large sheets.

GLASS-BLOWING TERMS

Glass-blowers use a variety of special terms. Here are a few:
• gather: a blob of glass collected on the end of a blowpipe;
• glory hole: an opening in a small furnace used to reheat glass;
• marver: a metal plate on which a gather is rolled and shaped;
• parison: the first bubble at the end of a blowpipe;
• pontil (or punty): a solid iron rod used to hold or shape soft glass.

RECYCLE RECYCLE RECYCLE RECYCLE

USING WASTE GLASS

Recycled glass can be used both for glass-blowing and the float-glass process. Broken or waste glass – which is called **cullet** – is added to the glass-making mixture. To make fine glass, the manufacturer has to make sure that the cullet is free of dirt or any other **impurities**.

Making glass in a factory

The first glass factories opened during the early twentieth century. More and more people wanted to buy glass containers, windows and other objects, so manufacturers looked for quicker, cheaper ways of making them. Machines were expensive to make, but once they were running, they lowered the cost of the finished glass.

Red-hot glass is shaped into wine bottles by the blow and blow method.

Bottles and jars

Glass containers are easy to make in large quantities in moulds. First metal moulds are made to exactly the right shape. The glass is heated to 1050-1200°C in a furnace. As the stream of molten glass flows to the bottle-making machine, it is automatically cut into small pieces called gobs.

Each gob is dropped into an empty (or blank) mould and a burst of air is pumped into it to shape the runny glass into a cylinder. While it is still hot, the glass cylinder is flipped over and drops into a second, bottle-shaped mould. Another blast of air blows the glass to the sides of the mould to give it its final bottle shape.

Then the bottle passes through cooling stages, where the glass hardens as it loses heat. This is called the blow and blow method.

Pressed glass

In 1825 an American inventor named John P Bakewell developed the first glass-pressing machine. This shaped objects such as bowls and dishes, giving them designs at the same time. First the machine dropped a hot gob of glass into a mould. Then a **plunger** pressed down on it quickly, so the runny glass spread around the inside of the mould. When the plunger was removed, the glass had taken on the shape of the mould. In 1827 the American glass maker Deming Jarves began producing glassware decorated with lacy patterns. These were popular, and the same glass-pressing techniques are used today.

Pipes, rods and tubes

Molten glass from the furnace is made into long thin pieces of glass by drawing the glass into a spinning hollow pipe. This is called a mandrel. Air blows the glass through

The pressed-glass technique makes very attractive tableware.

PRESS AND BLOW

Another container-making method is called press and blow. The first cylinder of glass is pressed into a blank mould by a metal plunger. From then on, the system is the same as blow and blow.

the mandrel, which turns it into a long, continuous tube of glass. This tube is then cut into lengths.

The beauty of glass

As well as being useful and practical, glass has been valued by artists and designers for centuries because of its beauty. Glass beads are a cheaper alternative to gemstones. Opaque and coloured glass are used for decoration. Glassware can also be cut and etched so that it looks beautiful, as well as serving a practical purpose.

Part of a beautiful Lalique glass panel at the Ritz Hotel in London.

DECORATIVE GLASS

The French jeweller René Lalique (1860-1945) set up a glass factory in 1910. He developed a style of moulded glass, decorating it with realistic patterns and beautiful colours. Lalique was invited to decorate the interiors of buildings with glass columns and walls, and his work was displayed in churches and ocean liners. His amazing designs were shown at the Paris Exhibition in 1925 and made him famous. Lalique glass became the height of fashion.

Adding lead

Lead can be added to the glass-making mixture to produce clearer, shinier and more brilliant glass (see page 16). **Lead crystal** contains between 24 and 35 per cent (roughly a quarter to a third) lead oxide. One of the most important and attractive features of this fine glass is that it is more refractive. This means it bends light more than other glass, giving it more flashing brilliance or sparkle. For this reason, lead crystal is often used for jewellery and ornaments.

Cut glass

Glass can also be decorated by grinding and engraving it with lines, designs and patterns. This produces cut glass. First a craftsman takes the piece to be cut – such as a goblet – and marks a pattern on it with a revolving steel grinding wheel or a small drill. The cuts can be smoothed and polished by running them past a sandstone wheel.

Etching and sandblasting

Glass objects can be given a design or a different look by frosting, which makes parts of them translucent or semi-opaque. This is done by covering any parts to be left transparent and then etching or **sandblasting** a translucent pattern on the rest. An acid is used to etch glass, or a compressed-air gun can blast coarse sand against the glass, leaving a rough surface.

This lead-crystal owl was made by the Swarovski glass company.

CRYSTAL ORNAMENTS

Daniel Swarovski (1862-1956) was the son of an Austrian glass cutter. In 1895 he founded a company that is still famous for its ornamental glass. Today the company makes crystal figurines and miniatures, fashion jewellery, home decoration and chandeliers. Some of the glass it makes is coated with metallic chemicals, giving the surface a colour or a rainbow effect.

Speciality glass

Today glass is used in a wide range of different ways. For example, cooks need heat-resistant glassware that they can put in the oven. Opticians need glass for a variety of different spectacles, including some that become sunglasses in bright light. Scientists and glass specialists have developed special glass for these and many other uses.

Boiling an egg in a heat-resistant Pyrex saucepan.

Flint and lead

During the seventeenth century, English glass maker George Ravenscroft (1618-81) added a mineral called black flint to his glass formula. His flint crystalline glass was clear and brilliant, and it became stronger and lasted better when he replaced the flint with a lead oxide called red lead. Others soon copied Ravenscroft, who put a raven's head seal on his glassware. Lead glass became the most popular type of fine glassware. Today we usually call this lead crystal glass (see page 14) or soda-lead glass.

NON-RECYCLABLE

Pyrex and other special types of glass cannot be recycled with ordinary bottles and jars. That's because they have different ingredients and melt at a higher temperature, so they would cause lumps in the recycled molten glass. Most recycling units do not accept Pyrex cookware, drinks glasses, light bulbs, mirrors or window glass.

RECYCLE RECYCLE RECYCLE RECYCLE

In the oven and the lab

Glass is made heat-resistant by adding boric oxide, which is a form of the chemical **element boron**. When it is heated, this glass expands only about a third as much as soda-lime glass, so it can withstand high temperatures without cracking. This makes it suitable for ovenware and scientific laboratory equipment, such as test tubes and thermometers.

At the end of the nineteenth century, a German glass maker called Otto Scott (1851-1935) used the brand name Duran for his glass. In 1915, the US Corning Glass Works called their version Pyrex, and this is still a well-known trademark. One great advantage of ovenproof glassware is that a cook can see how the food is cooking, because the container is see-through.

Reacting to sunlight

During the 1960s opticians began to make spectacles which were also sunglasses. They used lenses made of **photochromic** glass, which darkens when strong sunlight passes through it. This happens because the **ultraviolet** (UV) **rays** in sunlight have a darkening effect on tiny particles of a substance called **silver chloride** in the glass. Once the glass is moved out of bright sunlight it lightens again. Today, most photochromic spectacle lenses are made of plastic. But glass is still used for tinted windows and instrument controls.

REFLECTING GLASS

Mirrors are made of high-quality glass. In sixteenth-century Murano (see pages 8-9), the Venetians added a sheet of **mercury** to the reverse side of the glass. Today, most mirror manufacturers use silver or aluminium instead. First the glass is polished and cleaned. Then the reverse is coated with the reflective metal.

Large mirrors with elaborate frames were popular in Victorian drawing rooms.

Making glass safer

One of the problems with glass is that it can be dangerous when it breaks. A drinking glass shatters into sharp pieces if it is hit or dropped. Glass splinters can cut people. But now glass can be specially made and treated so that it breaks into blunt, rounded pieces instead. This is called safety glass and there are several different types.

The safety glass in this car windscreen has shattered but still stayed in place.

Laminated for windscreens

The first safety glass was invented in the early 1900s by a French artist and scientist named Edouard Bénédictus (1878-1930). He invented safety glass by sticking a sheet of transparent plastic material between two pieces of glass. If one of the sheets of glass shattered, the broken pieces were held together by the plastic layer rather than flying in all directions. This glass is very useful for car windscreens, which crack into a spider-web pattern when hit by a stone. Today a **resin** called polyvinyl butyral (or **PVB**) is used for the plastic layer of **laminated** (or layered) glass. Heat and pressure are used to press the layers together, and the safety glass ends up looking like a single sheet of glass.

Toughened for doors

Glass can be toughened by **tempering** it, which means heating it to very high temperatures before cooling it. Glass sheets are heated to about 650°C and then chilled suddenly. This treatment increases the strength of the glass. Tempered glass is used for doors, skylights (roof windows) and the side and back windows of cars. It looks like ordinary glass, but can be many times stronger. When it breaks, tempered glass makes dull-edged pieces.

Bullet-proof

Glass makers call bullet-proof glass bullet-resistant, because they cannot be certain that any glass will resist all kinds of bullets fired at close range. This kind of glass is usually thick, multilayered laminated glass that cannot be penetrated by most bullets or by a hammer or an axe. There may be four or more plastic layers between glass sheets, and each piece of glass may be up to 25 mm thick. This glass is used in banks, security and military vehicles.

ONE-WAY PROTECTION

Security glass makers have created a bullet-resistant glass that works just one way. In a van, for example, the new security glass will stop bullets being fired from the outside but allow bullets to be fired through it from inside. Security companies are very interested in this new development.

Security vehicles like this one are used to deliver and collect money and valuables from banks. They are usually fitted with bullet-proof windows.

19

Fibres of glass

Molten glass can be formed into fibres, or threads which can be thinner than human hair. These threads are bendy and yet stronger than steel. Glass fibres do not stretch, rot or catch fire. Because of these useful properties, manufacturers use them for many different purposes.

A worker checks glass fibres at a factory in France.

Making fibres

Glass fibres are made by heating molten glass in a furnace (see pages 10-11). The molten glass then flows through hundreds of tiny holes in a metal shape called a **bush**. The strands of glass move on to a spinning drum, which winds them on to **spools**. The drum spins faster than the glass flows and stretches it into longer, thinner threads.

One round glob of molten glass 10 mm across can be spun into 95 km of thin fibre in less than half an hour. High-speed winders then twist separate fibres into yarns of glass. Another method is to pour molten glass into a spinning shape with hundreds

RECYCLING FIBREGLASS

Recycled glass can be used to make fibreglass (GRP) and glass wool. But ordinary recycling units do not take used fibreglass. Specialist companies in Germany and Sweden break down fibreglass by cutting and crushing it, and the resulting material is used to make products such as car bumpers. A Japanese company has found a way to recycle used glass wool.

Fibreglass is a popular material for small boats.

DRESSING IN GLASS

In 1893 an American glass maker named Edward Drummond Libbey (1854-1925) showed a dress made of silky spun glass fibres at the World's Columbian Exposition in Chicago. A popular actress called Georgia Cayvan (1857-1906) wore the dress, and newspapers reported that this could be the next big fashion fad. But glass didn't catch on in the fashion world.

of holes, called a crown. As the streams of glass are flung out of the crown, a blast of steam breaks them up and throws them on to a conveyor belt. This takes the thin glass pieces on to a set of rollers, where they are pressed into a mat known as glass wool.

In 1938 American inventor Games Slayter (1896-1964) developed a new insulation material he called fibreglass. Today it is usually known as glass wool. It is good for keeping out heat and cold (see page 24) .

Adding glass to plastic

Glass fibres can be added to plastic material to strengthen it. The material is called glass-reinforced plastic (or GRP),

but people usually call it simply fibreglass. Manufacturers use it to make moulded plastic products, such as boats, car body parts and casing for electronic products.

Fine glass for lenses

The word optical refers to light, and optics is the scientific study of light. Optical glass is extremely high quality glass, and is used to make spectacle lenses, microscopes, telescopes, camera lenses and scientific instruments.

Lenses and prisms

Lenses are pieces of curved and polished glass that refract (or bend) light as it passes through them. In this way they focus light on to an object, such as the human eye. Glass has played an important part in the history of optics, which scientists such as Galileo Galilei (1564-1642) and Isaac Newton (1642-1727) began to study hundreds of years ago. Newton found that when beams

A bundle of optical fibres. Each fibre carries light all along its length.

of sunlight passed through a glass **prism** the beams split into the colours of the rainbow.

Carrying information

Glass fibres similar to those used for fibreglass (see page 20) are used to transmit information as pulses of light and can carry

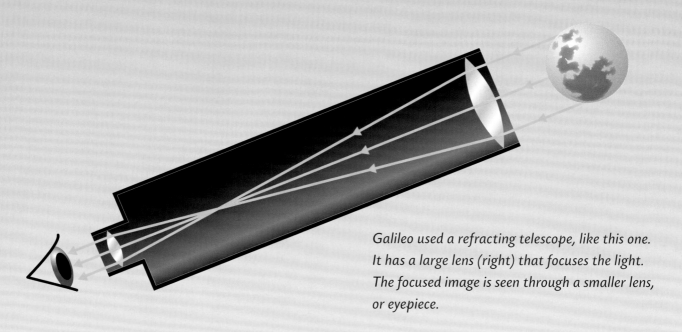

Galileo used a refracting telescope, like this one. It has a large lens (right) that focuses the light. The focused image is seen through a smaller lens, or eyepiece.

telephone, television and broadband signals. A single **optical fibre** is made of two parts – core and cladding. The core is a glass fibre, which is surrounded by a different kind of glass cladding (just as plastic surrounds the wire of an electrical cable). As light travels along the core, it bounces off the cladding and stays inside the core. Optical fibres can be grouped together into cables.

Flashes of light

Optical fibres carry flashes of light in the same way as metal wires carry pulses of electricity. The light flashes are transmitted at one end of the optical fibre by a **laser**, which uses a digital code to send information by flashing on and off at very high speed.

The code can represent text, pictures or voices, and light from many lasers can be sent together down a single optical fibre. This creates streams of **data** that can be

decoded by a receiver, which converts the message back to its original form. The message might be a phone call, a TV programme or Internet pages.

INVISIBLE GLASS AND PLASTIC

Glass reflects light as well as refracting it. During the 1940s American manufacturers developed what they called 'invisible glass' to make better spectacle lenses. They coated the lenses with a chemical film that cut down the amount of light reflected by the glass. This allowed more light to pass through the glass, and was also very useful in camera lenses. Today, coated plastic is often used instead.

Saving energy

Today we are all aware of the environmental problems facing our planet. They include air pollution and global warming. Much of our energy is generated by burning fossil fuels (coal, gas and oil), and this adds to our problems. So we need to save as much energy as we can.

One way of saving energy is to use energy-efficient cookers, fridges and washing machines. Glass plays an important part in these and it can also help to insulate our homes and save electricity in lighting.

Keeping heat in

One of the simplest ways to save energy is to insulate lofts. Without insulation about 15 per cent of the heat in a house goes straight through the roof. The best insulation is glass wool (see page 21), which comes in large rolls. It has lots of air between the strands of glass, which adds to the insulating effect. Glass wool can be used in roofs, walls and floors. A similar product called glass foam is made in moulds packed with crushed glass. They can be cut with a saw, but must be installed by an expert wearing a mask, because they may give off fine particles.

This man is checking the thickness of glass-wool insulation in a roof space.

Doubling up

Many modern windows have two panes of glass instead of one, with a thin gap between the panes. The air in this gap acts as a heat and sound insulator. This double-glazing keeps heat in and noise out. The Energy Saving Trust says that badly insulated window frames and single-glazed windows can lose up to a fifth of the heat in a home.

Energy-saving light bulbs come in different shapes and sizes.

A good thing?

One advantage of glass wool is that it can be made from recycled glass (see page 26). But environmentalists say that making glass wool uses a lot of energy, and as it is not biodegradable it cannot be disposed of easily. This is why it lasts so well for so long.

New style light bulbs

New energy-saving light bulbs use a different technology from traditional bulbs. But both are made of glass. The new bulbs are called compact fluorescent lamps (CFLs). An electric current passes through gas in a glass tube, making the tube's coating glow brightly. Old-fashioned incandescent bulbs are lit by a current passing through a wire that heats up and produces light. The new bulbs save energy because they last about ten times longer and use up to 80 per cent less electricity. Some of the new bulbs have strange shapes, which are easy to make from glass.

Recycling glass

Glass is easy to recycle and reuse. We can recycle it again and again and it will still be as good as new. Recycling glass bottles and jars into new containers helps the environment in several ways.

The more glass we recycle, the less glass we throw away in landfill dumps. Recycling also means we use less raw materials to make new glass, so there is less quarrying and less damage to the environment. We also use less energy to recycle glass than to make new glass, so factories give off fewer harmful waste gases.

Bottle banks

Bottles and jars for recycling can be put into bottle banks. Most neighbourhoods have bottle banks, and many collect glass for recycling in separate bins. Bottle banks have different slots for clear, brown and green (or blue) glass. This makes it easier to reuse the glass, because if all the colours were mixed together, the new bottles would be a dull, muddy colour. All glass bottles and jars can be recycled, but items made from different kinds of glass should not be put in the bottle bank. You should not put glass cups, bowls or jugs; light bulbs or electronic-equipment glass; window panes; or heat-resistant glass ovenware (such as Pyrex) into bottle banks.

You may find a bottle bank outside your local supermarket. Shoppers can recycle their old bottles before buying new ones.

Different colours of crushed glass are kept separate at the recycling plant.

How is glass recycled?

Waste glass is taken to a recycling plant, where the used bottles and jars are crushed into small pieces in a crusher or mill. The crushed glass is called cullet. This is taken to the furnace of a glass-making factory and used as a new raw material.

Recycled glass is remelted on its own or along with other raw materials (see page 4), to make new glass. Crushed cullet can also be used in other ways. It can be used to make roads, to manufacture bricks or to produce **ceramics**.

RECYCLE RECYCLE RECYCLE RECYCLE

ENERGY SAVINGS

Every tonne of recycled glass used to make new bottles prevents 315 kg of carbon dioxide from being pumped out of the chimneys of glass factories. It takes 1.2 tonnes of raw materials to make 1 tonne of new glass, but only 1 tonne of recycled glass. Recycling one glass bottle saves enough energy to power:

• a 60-watt light bulb for 100 minutes;
• a computer for 25 minutes;
• a washing machine for 10 minutes.

Glass in the future

Today there is no shortage of the raw materials we use to make glass. We now recycle more and more used glass and we should be able to go on making and using glass in future. Scientists will continue to invent new uses for glass. Perhaps later this century, people will be wearing glass-fibre clothing or using glass for interior flooring, staircases or large structures, such as bridges.

Creating energy

Elements such as the silvery metal neodymium can be added to the glass-making mix to create laser glass. Some lasers use this form of glass to send light through crystals of glass. Researchers are experimenting with a process that uses a powerful glass laser to concentrate its beams on hydrogen atoms so that the nuclei at their centre fuse (or combine). This nuclear fusion releases huge amounts of energy in the form of heat, which can be used to create electricity. If it proves practical and safe, this form of nuclear power might become important in future.

Glass city

At an international architectural exhibition in 2008, designers revealed plans for a futuristic city of glass. They plan to cover 2.3 square kilometres

This 180-metre tall building in London, nicknamed the Gherkin, has 24,000 square metres of glass on its outside.

with a giant glass pyramid that could house up to one million people. The development is called the Ziggurat (after an ancient pyramid-shaped tower). Inside, people will need very little energy in their daily lives. The glass city will be environmentally friendly – it will have no cars and will be powered by wind turbines. A monorail transport system will take people wherever they want to go. The city will have parks, water channels and lakes with climate zones that become cooler as you rise higher. If the experiment is successful, glass cities could spring up all over the world.

New kinds of glass?

Researchers, scientists and glass manufacturers have been inventing and developing new kinds of glass for centuries. This will continue during the present century and beyond. They may invent types of glass that no one has thought of before, for

This is an artist's idea of what the Ziggurat glass city will look like.

GLASS CITIES

The Ziggurat glass city will use glass to keep the temperature even inside. This type of building, called a biosphere, has been tested before but was not a great success. Space agencies are researching similar ideas to find out whether humans could go and live on other planets such as Mars.

example glass which is stronger than any yet made, or or even completely unbreakable glass. Or they might come up with a type of glass which changes colour, as well as darkening when exposed to bright light.

Glossary

air pollution Damage to the air caused by harmful substances.

archaeologist A person who studies the ancient past by digging up and looking at remains.

blowpipe A metal tube used to shape molten glass.

boron A non-metallic chemical element that is usually prepared as a brown powder.

bush A metal part in a machine with a round hole or many holes.

carbon dioxide (or CO_2) A greenhouse gas that is given off when fossil fuels (such as coal, oil or gas) are burned.

ceramics Pots and other objects made from heated, hardened clay; pottery.

chandelier A hanging set of lights decorated with glass and with branches for holding light bulbs or candles.

costume jewellery Inexpensive jewellery made from glass rather than gemstones.

crystalline glass Very clear, sparkling glass.

cullet Broken or waste glass used for recycling.

data Information that can be sent along a cable in the form of pulses of electricity or light.

element A substance that cannot be separated into a simpler form.

etch To cut a design into a surface using a sharp point or acid.

figurine A small ornamental figure.

furnace An oven-like structure in which materials can be heated to very high temperatures.

gemstone A precious stone that is cut and polished for use in jewellery.

global warming Heating up of the Earth's surface, especially caused by pollution from burning fossil fuels.

gob A lump of soft glass.

guild An association of craftspeople in medieval Europe, which set standards and made regulations.

impurity An unwanted substance, such as dirt, that could lower the quality of glass.

laminated glass A glass sheet made up of separate layers of glass and plastic.

laser A device that sends out an intense beam of light.

lead crystal Glass that contains lead oxide to make it more brilliant.

limestone A rock formed from the skeletons and shells of prehistoric marine creatures.

mercury A silver-white metal that remains liquid at room temperature.

mould A hollow container that gives shape to a molten substance when it hardens.

obsidian A glass-like volcanic rock that was used in prehistoric times for making tools.

opaque Describing a material that cannot be seen through.

optical fibre A thin thread of glass through which light can be sent to carry information.

oxide A substance made up of oxygen and another element; metallic oxides add colour to glass.

photochromic glass Glass that becomes darker when more light passes through it.

plunger Part of a machine that presses something with force.

prism A solid piece of glass with three-sided ends that separates light into colours.

PVB Short for polyvinyl butyral, a plastic used to stick layers of glass together.

refract To bend light.

resin A substance that is used to make plastic objects.

saltpetre A salty mineral (also called potassium nitrate) that can be used to preserve meat.

sandblast To mark or clean a material by blasting it with air or steam mixed with sand.

silicon dioxide A hard mineral that melts at a very high temperature; also called silica sand.

silver chloride A light-coloured compound that goes darker when it is exposed to light.

soda ash A white compound used in making glass and soap; also called sodium carbonate.

spool A cylinder (or reel) around which fibres can be wound.

temper To toughen glass by heating it to a very high temperature and then cooling it.

ultraviolet rays Rays in sunlight with a shorter wavelength than visible light rays.

vessel A container used to hold liquids.

Websites

Information and news on glass recycling, including what you can do to help.
http://www.wasteonline.org.uk/resources/InformationSheets/glass.htm#4

An association set up to spread knowledge of glass and glass making.
http://www.glassassociation.org.uk/

The International Guild of Glass Artists encourages the use of glass in art, including tips and techniques.
http://www.igga.org/

Information on Murano glass from Venice, its history and manufacture today.
http://www.venetian-glass.info/

Brief history of glass with a timeline.
http://www.glassonline.com/infoserv/history.html

Index